HOW TO CREATE A BUSINESS PLAN LENDERS WILL LOVE

DAVID L BROWN
BUSINESS PLAN ANSWER MAN

DBROWN & COMPANY LLC

ISBN-978-0-9850460-6-4

Library of Congress Control Number: 2018675309 Printed in the United States of America

"My experience with David Brown Company has been more than awesome. He has written a business plan for me to be able to get an SBA loan for my restaurant that was more than adequate and showed his vast knowledge and experience with these matters, so I recommend him for anybody that needs as such. David Brown is a very well-mannered and helpful man; he will meet all of the requirements of and body's financial institution regarding loans. I highly recommend him for any kind of research and documentation that anyone needs."

-Bill Shunia, - Bill's Bistro & Pappa Sofano Pizzaria

"Thank you, David, for helping me develop a more focused approach to my business. With your insightful plan, I was able to double my profits without doubling my workload! What a blessing!"

- Dave Crabill, - Owner, Eclectic Sales & Creative Marketing, LLC

"David has always given me great advice and suggestions that have helped me become more confident in starting and growing my business. He has also given me ideas for my business that I didn't even know were possible or existed. And, of course, he did a great job on my business plan. Thank you so much, David!"

-Stacey Holman, - The Crafting Nook LLC

"I want to take a moment to say a big "thank you!"

Recently I began the treacherous road of purchasing a building to expand my business along with applying for a business loan - yikers!

I honestly had no idea how to prepare a proper business plan to present to the bank, so I read David's book *From the Bottom Up* and with his help, the bank said yes!

Not only did they say yes, but they also complemented me on my business plan! Thank you from the bottom of my heart for writing this book and for your guidance! You are making a difference in people's lives and in our community ."

-Becky, Owner of Mamie & Mossie's Gal

"I am so excited; my life things have been prompted by David Brown's book, *From the Bottom Up*. He has this awesome thing on his website that you just fill in the blanks for your business plan. I've been dreading the business plan part for my entire career and had bits and pieces, but the way he puts it together makes me so excited."

-Wendy Schweifler, - CEO and Founder Bod-E-Nomics

Foreword

You've had an "aha" moment when this great business idea pops into your head. You're thinking," I need to do this." Then another thought pops into your head: "How do I take this idea in my head, write it out, and implement it?" Do you just say forget it or fumble your way through the process?

Sound familiar? If it does, you're not alone. Many businesses have started this same way: Struggling through the process like stumbling through the dark, bumping into every obstacle you possibly can. I have heard this from a variety of business owners.

Part of any business idea is figuring out if you can start a business without borrowing money. There are many who can, while others need capital. Are you one of the businesses that needs startup or working capital? If so, next comes the thought of where the money will come from and what you need to do to get it.

There are a few things you need to do in order to get a loan. They are:

- Knowledge of what the loan is for.
- A solid business plan.
- Business licenses and other legal documents.
- How much money you need to borrow?
- A plan on how to repay the loan

Throughout this book these items are addressed. One of the goals of this book is to help you be prepared if you need to obtain funding. I want to help minimize the time between applying and receiving the loan proceeds. This happens by spending the necessary time to build a solid plan and put all of the necessary documents together that address the issues above, and more.

This book has information to help you prepare for obtaining financing for your business. I have dedicated a chapter to financing to provide you with the knowledge about what lenders are looking for and requiring, while providing you with the knowledge as you interview lenders to find the best option for you and your business.

Preparing you for the loan process and creating a solid business plan is going to make it easier for the lender to fall in love with your business. They will see the passion that you bring forward and understand that the same passion will carry forward into starting and running that business.

Another goal of this book is to help the new business owner take the thought from his/her head, decide if it's a viable business idea, and provide that business owner with a track to follow as they start to build a business, while answering questions, along the way. During my career as an entrepreneur and business owner I have run into many obstacles by learning the hard way and I want to help you avoid them.

Going through the process may have you scratching your head and thinking, "Is it worth it?" There are questions and topics that require some deep thinking and possibly discussions with a partner, spouse/significant other, or a trusted friend. The more thought you put in on the front end, the more time and aggravation saved later.

The book is broken down into pieces, each of which include steps needed to increase your success rate. There may be some sections that don't apply to your type of business, but I urge you to still read through them rather than skipping over them. A topic may trigger a thought that will help you. If so, make a note of it and keep going.

Are you ready to dig in? Let's go!

Table of Contents

Chapter 1: The Idea

You've had an "aha" moment! You know what I'm talking about: suddenly, the light bulb above your head turns on and you think, "Wow, that's a great idea." One of the ideas may be starting your own business or starting a business may even be a dream of yours. Either way, you need to transport the thoughts in your head to paper and decide how you will build a business around them.

In this chapter we will go through a series of questions to determine if the idea will be a good business, hobby or a passing thought. I encourage you to write down the answers in the space below. As we move through the process of transporting your idea, the following information will be put to good use.

Describe your idea:

_____

_____

_____

_____

_____

_____

_____

Why do you believe this is a good idea for
starting a business?

_____

_____

_____

_____

_____

_____

_____

Why do I want to start a business?

_____

_____

_____

_____

_____

_____

_____

What do you picture in your mind the
business looking like?

_____

_____

_____

_____

_____

_____

_____

What do you want out of the business?

_____

_____

_____

_____

_____

_____

_____

How much money do you need to make to
support you and my family?

_____

_____

What will make your business different from
any other business with a similar product or
service?

_____

_____

_____

_____

_____

_____

_____

What amount of time are you prepared to invest in starting and running a business?

_____

_____

How much money do you have to invest in starting and running a business?

_____

_____

Are you prepared to make this investment of time and money? _____

What does your ideal customer look like for your product/service? (Be specific!)

_____

_____

_____

_____

_____

_____

_____

_____

_____

_____

_____

_____

_____

_____

Is there a large enough pool of people that meet these criteria to support a business?

_____

_____

Where will you find this group of people?

_____

_____

_____

_____

_____

_____

_____

Will you need help to start and run your

business? If yes, who?

Who are your advisors?

Attorney: _____

Accountant: _____

Consultants: _____

Mentors: _____

_____

_____

Others: _____

_____

_____

How much and what kind of experience do you have running a business?

_____

_____

_____

_____

_____

_____

_____

How much time and money will it take to start your business?

_____

_____

_____

_____

_____

_____

_____

Where will your business be located?

_____

_____

_____

If you need money to start your business

where will you get it?

_____

_____

_____

_____

_____

_____

If you need to help getting started where will you find it?

David Brown, Business Plan Answer Man

dave@businessplananswerman.com

Chapter 2: Decisions

You provided a lot of information to get your mind going in the last chapter. Now it's time to look at what, why and how as it pertains to your business idea.

It's time to make the BIG decision: press onward or scrap the idea. It sounds harsh, but that's the bottom line. Moving forward will take time and investment to get you where you want to go.

There's nothing wrong with taking the time to talk it out with yourself or others. You have to make sure that this is what you want to do. If your spouse or significant other is not on board, it will be even harder to move forward. Be sure you are both on the same page, that way they will be your sounding board for ideas and actions you will take.

The answers to the questions in chapter one, if your spouse/significant other wasn't involved in making those decisions, now is a good time to review together. Your investment of time and money will affect your family time and budget.

I guarantee your spouse or significant other will be the one who you blow off steam to when you're frustrated because something isn't going like you want it to.

As you press on, we will have more decisions that you need to make.

Think about the name of your business - any ideas? Once you have an idea, the next step is to make sure no one else is uses that business name. When picking a name, don't make it too long, as you will want to have it as a domain name for your website and email. Make it easy to remember and spell to avoid confusion for your clients/customers.

Personally, I like to start with a Google search to see what's being used, whether it's the name I prefer or something similar. Sometimes a slight variation of the name you like may have to be used.

The next thing to do is to go to your Secretary of State's website to check the official registry for the name. You should find an entity search, and this is where you would register for a Limited Liability Company (LLC) or a Corporation (Inc). If you just want a Doing

Business As (DBA) that is usually done with your county clerk's office. We will discuss more about each option as we go along.

If your Google and Secretary of State searches didn't show the company name that you want , then it's time, check that name's availability as a domain. You can use a service such as www.GoDaddy.com or a variety of hosting companies like www.BlueHost.com or www.Hostgator.com to purchase the domain. The cost varies on which service you use. You will find a name search on these sites, search for the name you would choose as a .com. This is preferable the most widely recognized of all the options.

I advised you to not make your business name too long, and here is why: using an email address with your own domain name, such as dave@businessplananswerman.com,   this does a few things. First of all, it looks professional and shows that you're invested in your business by not using a generic email account. Secondly, every time you send an email, your company name is in front of the person's face. If you have too long of a name, people may not remember it when they go to search for you.

If both the business name and domain name are available, then great. Before going ahead and filing for both and spending money there's another decision to make: What type of entity will your business be? There are several options and you to decide which is best for you. I recommend consulting with your attorney and accountant because each option has its own requirements, and they may be good advisers in this situation.

Here are brief descriptions of each to give you an idea. This is purely informational, as I am neither an attorney nor an accountant.

There are four types of entities:
- Sole Proprietor
- Partnership
- Limited Liability Company (LLC)
- Corporation (two types S and C)

Without proper advice you may end up with the wrong business type, which could hurt you down the road. Let's look at information on each type.

SOLE PROPRIETOR

This is the most basic form of entity.

You own the company and are responsible for all assets and liabilities and the income/loss statements are reported on your personal tax return

Advantages:

- Easy and inexpensive to form
- Have complete control

Disadvantages:

- Unlimited personal liability
- Harder to obtain funding
- Heavy burden on owner

PARTNERSHIP

This is a single business with two or more people sharing ownership. Each partner contributes to all assets of business including money, skills, and labor in return for a share of the profits/losses.

Types:

- **General Partnership**: All profits, liabilities and management duties are divided equally according to shares in the partnership agreement.

- **Limited Partnership:** More complex than general and allows partners to limit input into partnership decisions.
- **Joint Venture:** Acts as a general partnership but only for a single project and limited period of time.

Forming a partnership

- Choose a business name
- Register your business
- Obtain business licensing and permits
- Register with the IRS

Advantages:

- Easy and less expensive than other business forms
- Shared financial commitment among partners
- Complimentary skill sets with partners

Disadvantages:

- Joint and individual liability
- Potential disagreement among partners
- Shared profits

LIMITED LIABILITY COMPANY (LLC)

This type of company provides limited liability and is taxed as a sole proprietor or partnership.

Requirements:

- Choose business name
- File articles of organization
- Create an operating agreement
- Obtain licensing or permits

Advantages:

- Limits personal liability for business actions
- Less recordkeeping than corporations
- Fewer restrictions on sharing profits

Disadvantages:

- Limited life when changing members
- Considered self-employed and subject to self-employment taxes

CORPORATIONS

<u>C-CORP</u>
This is an independent legal entity owned by shareholders the corporation itself is responsible for all business actions, assets, and liabilities.

<u>Requirements:</u>
- Choose business name
- Register the business as a corporation
- Obtain any licensing and permits

<u>Advantages:</u>
- Limited liability – personal assets are protected
- Ability to generate capital
- Corporate tax treatment
- Attractive to potential employees

<u>Disadvantages:</u>
- Costly and time consuming to start and operate
- Double taxation
- Additional paperwork – highly regulated

S – CORP

Provides the protection of a C-Corp except that is taxed a Limited Liability Company.

Requirements:

- Must determine if qualified under IRS rules before filing
- Same general requirements as C Corp

Advantages:

- Tax savings – no corporate taxes – taxed on personal return
- Business expenses tax credits – some expenses can be written off
- Independent life – continues after death of a shareholder

Disadvantages:

- Stricter operational process
- Shareholder compensation requirement
- Additional paperwork

After working with your advisors and determining what needs to be filed and how to keep records for your new business, it's time to secure the name and domain. The requirements may vary from state to state.

Does your business need any special licenses to operate? This can vary from state to state and municipality to municipality.

Depending on your business type and where you are operating from there may be permits required for occupancy or zoning requirements. Make sure you check these out.

These issues sometime deter people from moving forward as it takes some time to set up your business entity properly.

Chapter 3: Your Business Plan

One of the frequently asked questions I hear is, "Why do I need a business plan - it's just me?" The more experienced entrepreneurs add to that, "I know how to run a business," or "My plan is in my head, I don't need to write it out."

Every day we are exposed to over 5000 marketing messages, add to that your daily life and personal issues you may have. I don't know about you but for me, any business ideas in my head would be gone quickly and there goes my business plan. It is proven that if you can commit something to writing it has a higher probability of happening. We learned this in school; remember writing out our spelling words every week? This was so we could remember them, and your business plan is no different.

The other reason you need a business plan is to obtain funding to start and/or operate your business. If you approach a potential lender about borrowing money for a business without a business plan, the first thing you may hear is "Come back when you have a plan." The business plan will contain the information that they need to know about what you plan to do and how you plan to repay the loan.

The business plan is your roadmap for your road to success. Knowing who, what, where, how, and why helps you stay focused and moving forward, not only for yourself, but also for any partners or staff you may have. When everyone is on the same page, things run smoother.

At my insurance agency I hired part-time people to run my marketing campaigns. They would track the results and provide reports on a regular basis. This took work off of my plate, allowing me to focus on high-income generating activities, sales.

The business plan is made up of smaller plans, some of them are the marketing plan, financial plan, goal planning, tracking system and possibly a staffing plan. Together they will tell a potential funder what they need to know about your business.

Understanding the need and importance of a business plan prepares us for the work to come. Another frequently asked question about a business plan is, "What's in a business plan?"

i will provide a brief summary of what is in each section of a business plan as well as some tips as we move forward. The plan will include details about the who, what, where, why, and how you will build and run your business. Here's a list of the sections of the plan:

- Cover Page
- Table of Contents
- Executive Summary
- Mission statement
- Vision statement
- Core Values
- Management Team
- Market Analysis
- Marketing Plan
- Budget(s)
- Goals

- Professional Development (if applicable)
- Appendix

Let's look at each section and provide what you need to include in each. For a more detailed look into business planning my book *From the Bottom Up: The Ultimate Guide for Business Planning to Profitability* is a step-by-step guide for creating your business plan.

Cover Page

The is the first impression of your business. It must be neat and professional and include some basic information. In the bottom left corner should be the business name, address, phone number, and website URL. A picture of your logo or brick and mortar building can be in the center to identify your business and brand.

Table of Contents

This is a basic item. Make sure all of the page numbers are correct in regard to the location of the information of the plan.

Executive Summary

This is a critical piece of the plan. It must describe the business and how you will make the money to repay the funder for the loan you receive. This should be no longer than ONE page. My recommendation to my clients is to do this last. Why? You may have a vision of the business, but the details have yet to be created. Once you have all of the pieces it helps paint a bigger picture in your mind and helps you to convey that in a few paragraphs.

Mission Statement

This is a brief statement of why you are in business. What is your purpose?

Vision Statement

Break out the crystal ball. What do you see your business looking like in the future? Future here is 20 years plus. Be specific.

Core Values

What are the guiding principles in your life and those you will guide your business? Make this one or two paragraphs.

Management Team

What is the business structure? Describe who is doing what task(s). For instance, you may be the CEO/salesperson. There may be someone else doing the books. Do you have key people not in the management structure? You should include the resume for each in the appendix along with an organization chart, if applicable.

Market Analysis

What is the market for your product or service? Who is the competition? What makes your company different from them? Who is your preferred customer? describe them in detail. Where will you find them? In the beginning we discussed this information before deciding if a business was the right thing for you.

Marketing Plan

You have identified your preferred customer and where you will find them, now it's time to look at how you will reach them. What is the best method for contacting them? What is the media formats you will use?

Build a 12-month marketing calendar. What are you going to focus on each month? January is a new year, February you have Valentine's Day, March is Spring and so on. Focus on how your product or service will fill a need for your customer around the topics you identify for each month.

Dan Kennedy, one of the most successful copywriters describes the ideal marketing plan as the right message, with the right media to the right customer.

Budget(s)

Money is key to operating the business. Start with a monthly budget, and once you have that annualize it. Frequently this is where many business owners stop. A lender will want to see a three-year financial plan.

The (s) is there if you are a new business and require startup funding. A lender will also want to see your startup costs, which are generally onetime expenses to open the doors. Include at least three months of operating revenue to get up and running.

Goals

Describe your one, three and five-year goals. The goals should be SMART: Specific, Measurable, Achievable, Realistic and Time bound. Make sure the goals track with your budget and financial projections.

Professional Development (applicable)

You may or may not have professional licensure requirements. There may be skills that you need or wish to learn to allow you to better operate your business. If you're hiring employees, you may wish to learn more about human resources. Bookkeeping skills are always helpful. Whatever you wish to learn, describe it here. This shows the reader you are committed to improving yourself to grow the business.

Appendix

This is the place for all of your supporting documents to the pieces of your plan, like the management team resumes, estimates to substantiate the startup budget, industry standards for cost associated with your financial projections, etc. Provide a list to follow that with all the documents. Create a page that lists the documents included in the appendix in the order as they are in the plan.

Make sure that when your business plan is done have someone read it over and look for areas that don't make sense or are out of place along with typos.

After any adjustments are made, "fluff it and buff it," as they say. Either place it in a binder where you can showcase the cover sheet or have it combed. When you present this plan as stated it is the first impression of you and your business. It must look professional!

Chapter 4: Your Marketing Plan

In the business plan chapter, I talked about creating a marketing plan. In this chapter we will get into more of the nitty-gritty of building that plan.

Whether you are creating a side hustle or a full-time business, the information is the same. When to begin marketing and how aggressive you need to market or are you going to outsource the marketing are decisions you need to make as you begin the marketing plan.

Marketing begins before you even open the door for your new business. You've completed all of the work in preparation to open your business, so you need to set a target date to open that marks the beginning of the marketing. Did you buy or lease a building? Then you can begin at that time with some marketing. The pre-opening marketing is all about building interest in your product or service and making potential customers aware of your grand opening. All of this takes some planning.

Everyone knows social media is the current buzz in marketing. But before we get into that discussion you have to make sure it's right for your business. Get out your notes on who your ideal customer is. Are you a business-to-business (B2B) or a business-to-consumer (B2C)? The answer helps lead you to a proper platform. If you are B2B you may want to focus on LinkedIn, while B2C may focus on the Facebook and other individual platforms. Your ideal customer are ever changing when it comes to demographics so reviewing the effectiveness of your marketing on a regular basis is a must.

Back to the ideal client. If you are looking for a person who is a leading-edge baby boomer, they may not be a big user of social media. While millennials and Gen X individuals are almost certain to use social media. How the ideal customer groups you identified get their news and what their demographics look like are especially important. That's why it's important to be specific as you identified who your ideal customer is. You may have multiple groups if you have multiple products or services, so you will need to define each group per product or service. This applies to B2B and B2C.

The yellow pages, remember them? They are almost a thing of the past and were expensive to advertise in. *Google My Business (GMB)* the yellow pages of the internet as I refer to it as, where you need to be. Why? Think about this; When you look for something where are you looking? Google. To be found, you need a business page. Yet as valuable as this is, many businesses don't do it. I have seen the value of GMB page that I have built a company around it with the help of a partner, to create this listing and other social media marketing for other businesses- Pinnacle Media Group LLC. This is a free listing, it just a little time to set it up and take ownership of your company page. Take a look at the GMB page for Pinnacle Media Group LLC just by typing the name if Google search. Not only does this provide information about your business, but you also post photos of your work, testimonials from clients and submit updates of what is going on with tips to show your value to the reader.

Print marketing can be referred to as "above the fold" meaning that if you're looking at a newspaper, you would show up on the upper half of the front page. In internet searches the goal is to be on the first page. How many times do you look over the listings after the first page? Having the GMB that links to your website and other business items helps your search engine optimization (SEO). The better your SEO score, the higher in the rankings you are.

The goal of any marketing is to bring customers in the door. In order to do that, they need to know, like, and trust you. Building rapport with potential customers and letting them know what you do is critical. In the social media world, there are so many choices with more showing up online continuously. You don't need to be on everyone social media platform, pick two or three and focus on those. These need to be the ones that your ideal customers are on.

Whatever marketing you are doing be sure and track your return on investment. Online marketing through your website, social media sites, and Google My Business all have analytics you can install to track usage.

I can hear you now grumbling about this, saying doing who has time? Relax. There are companies out there that can do this for you. Above I mentioned Pinnacle Media Group LLC is one of those companies. If you wish to discuss this further, you can email our team at info@PinnacleMediaGroupLLC.com.

In the marketing section of the business plan, a marketing calendar was mentioned. My experience with this is that it's helpful to have a written plan on what you will do month-to-month, including multiple ways of connecting with your ideal customers. Tip: Don't forget about your existing customers once you have them. Part of your marketing plan should be continuous touches with them, at least monthly.

One of the first things you need to do is build a following or tribe. This is usually done by providing something of value in exchange for the coveted email address. You goal should be to build this list using a program other than social media. If you build your email list on social media platform, they own the list, (i.e. If your following list is only on Facebook, they could make a change and you could lose your list) There is a variety of platforms where this list building process can be automated, such as *Mail Chimp* and *Constant Contact*. These programs provide email campaigns, such as email newsletters or scheduled emails. Using this type of program, you own the list of clients. Once you build a list, you continue to connect with them on a regular basis which is commonly referred to as a drip marketing campaign.

I am in favor of a combination of online and offline marketing techniques. This could be something like a printed newsletter or direct mail along with the drip marketing campaign described above is great option if done correctly. Remember the comment from Dan Kennedy earlier? The right message, on the right media to the right people equals success.

That's why you have to determine how your ideal customer gets their news.

You have the idea of how and why to build a marketing calendar, now. Let's go back to the start of your marketing campaign. It's important to build interest in your business before opening the door. I want to share a story about one of my clients about this very thing. He contacted me about creating his business plan, during our initial discussion, his goal was to build his current side hustle into a full-time business. He has a full-time job currently with a side hustle of golf instruction. His goal to expand the golf instruction to include retail, using the connections he made in the golf world from his prior golfing career. He envisioned building this into a full-time business that would support him and employees.

Prior to us working together he had already secured agreements with a several manufacturers and suppliers to obtain inventory at a reduced cost. He needed to begin a social media campaign since he was after the golf enthusiast who wanted instruction and products including golf club repair. He began to post to various social media platforms on a regular basis about the products he had lined up, and with the help of a website builder, created a virtual store, with all these products. His posts were about how these products can help someone improve their golf game.

The social media campaign would then move over to LinkedIn, where you would find corporate executives, that may want to improve their golf game or maybe have their business sponsor a clinic for their staff.

Using this marketing tactic, my client is building a tribe of followers so when he opens his brick and mortar store, he already has a group of potential customers who are local and would use the physical store, keeping the virtual store to expand his reach.

What he did was build a platform to reach clients ahead of the physical store opening. It's all about making people aware of your business and showing how you can solve their problems.

When you produce marketing pieces and send them out tracking is key. If you send out a batch of hard copy marketing pieces and you have little to no return, don't quit! Adjust the message or double-check your list. Make one change at a time resend and check your return. Often times marketing is trial and error, so you must test and send

Marketing is also about building a recognizable brand. Think about the blimp flying over a sporting event, it doesn't say buy now. It says the brand name such as Goodyear or Met Life. Why? To be top of mind, so when you are ready to buy their product the name pops in your head.

Everything about your business affects your brand. These include, but are not limited to:

- Appearance of your marketing materials
- Professional quality of your business cards
- Look and feel of your building inside and out?
- Customer service
- Positive recommendations

- Reputation
- Quality of your product or service
- Social media presence

When it comes to marketing make sure you have money set aside for it. When times get tough the first thing that normally gets cut is marketing, which is a common mistake. You should be spending more on marketing to reach more people. If people don't hear about you they forget you even existed.

I moved my insurance agency to an opposite side of town. I went through the steps we described in the chapter of location.. The next thing I had to do was alert the masses of people in the area plus our current clients of our move, and we used a multimedia approach for this task.

We started by purchasing a mailing list of all households within half mile of the new location. Our goal was to make people aware that we were in their neighborhood. I designed an oversize postcard that was eye-catching and mailed these out over a two-week period. After they were mailed, I put a billboard ad up in the middle of the radius. It was a perfect location overlooking a gas station. When people were pumping gas there was the billboard with my picture staring down at them. Words of wisdom: If you put your picture on a billboard, prepare for harassment! I thought it was bad when friends and clients harassed me, but when the Pastor told me he was used to God looking down on him but the insurance guy not so much.

Throughout this marketing campaign I tracked all expenses. Within a week, a young lady came in carrying our postcard. When I finished her review, I ended up writing her insurance policies. When calculating the commission on the sale compared to our expenses, one client paid for the entire marketing campaign.

Chapter 5: Location Location Location

Sounds like the real estate industry, doesn't it? That is one of their slogans, but it applies to any business that's going to open a brick and mortar location.

Are you going to open an office or work from home? Some business owners are lucky, and they can work from home without the added expense of an office, while others need a physical location.

Picking a location has many factors to consider. Zoning can be an issue, so you must check with the municipal office to see what permitted uses are in the area. More factors to consider include what are the accessibility, parking, signage, and storage is?

If working in the home it's best to have a separate room for your business office. Check with your tax preparer to find out what is needed to deduct a home office on your taxes and your insurance company to find out about extra coverage for the office.

We're going to focus on a brick and mortar location for a bit. Scouting a location can be a daunting task. I remember what I went through just moving my insurance office years ago; I looked at so many locations that they all started to run together in my mind. As mentioned, zoning can be an issue and narrow your focus because, industrial, warehousing, manufacturing or storage facilities may only be allowed in a certain area.

Another thing to consider: Will your customers or potential customers be coming to visit your showroom or purchase goods or services? Accessibility and visibility are important factors to consider along with adequate parking for customers and staff. Is the location easy to get to? The zoning ordinance and building codes may limit your signage, so be sure check on all of these extra factors before securing your location.

Once you've narrowed the pool down to a couple of locations, you may want to talk to the landlord about the lease and what you would be responsible for. You will also want to discuss it with your attorney for any potential clauses that could have an adverse effect on you. You don't want to be surprised at the last minute!

Other areas to consider are:
- Are renovations needed? If so, what would be the cost and who would pay for them?
- Are there other costs associated with the lease?
- What will the insurance cost for the location and equipment?
- What is the cost of signage?
- How much inventory and furnishing will you need? Cost of these?
- What are the utility costs?
- What is the crime rate in the area?
- Will you need alarm system? Cost?
- Cost of operating license and permits?

Finding the right location is not simply as easy as finding a spot and saying. "I'll take it!" Do your homework ahead of time to save yourself headaches because, there are a lot of costs associated with a brick and mortar building. Some of these will fall into your startup budget while others will be in the operating budget, and some will be in both. There may also be deposits that fall into the startup budget for utilities.

Chapter 6: Who is Going to Help Me?

How many people do you need to run your business? Hiring people can be stressful, especially if you've never done it before, and having employees can be a challenge all by itself.

I want to share some things with you that hopefully will help you in the hiring process. The following are some questions for you to answer.

- How many people do you need to hire?
- Will they be full-time/part-time, or a combination?
- Will they be an employee or independent contractor? (Check the rules between the two.)
- What is the position you are hiring for?
- What is the job description for that position?
- Who will they report to?
- Who will train them?
- How much can you afford to pay?

- What is a competitive wage for this job/these jobs?
- What benefits if any can you afford to provide?
  - Health insurance
  - Paid holidays
  - Paid vacation
  - Retirement plan
- Have you considered other payroll costs?
  - Employers share of FICA
  - Employers share of Medicare
  - Unemployment Insurance (state and federal)
  - Workers compensation insurance
  - Cost to outsource payroll (if applicable)

If you aren't familiar with labor laws, I recommend you research appropriate hiring questions, otherwise you may find yourself in trouble with the law. Read up on the local, state, and federal employment laws and requirements. Establish a personnel file for each person you hire; record keeping is key and documents such as hire date, copies of forms signed, wages, disciplinary action, and performance reviews are important to keep.

While all the of the above are lessons learned, this is not official legal or financial advice, and I stress the importance of an attorney and accountant. There are firms such as Indeed and others who can do for a fee. Having spelled out in writing provides uniformity. Some advice I was given years ago that I will pass along is, "No matter how many employees you have 1 or 1000, act as if you were a large corporation." If you are coming out of the corporate world, think about the things the company you worked for had: an employee handbook, policies, and procedures, etc.

Your Certified Public Accountant (CPA) if they haven't obtained your Federal Employer Identification Number (EIN) will need it. You will need this number not only for banking purposes, but open unemployment insurance accounts (UIA) for the federal and state levels and income tax withholding accounts. Your

CPA can help you set up these accounts and help with payroll.

Research and investing time up front will save you later if something unfortunate were to occur. Don't be afraid to ask for help.

Chapter 7: Additional Considerations

Let's talk telephones. Are you using a landline? Your business will dictate what kind of phone you need like so many other decisions. Brick and mortar locations should have a landline. An office in the home- not so much. My cell phone is my primary number for the business, however, being old-school, I have never removed my landline. It's now used for conference calls, so I don't have to worry about the battery in my cell phone dying mid-call. If I had a true office phone in the house, it would be a separate line, because using a home phone as the business phone does not promote a professional appearance.

In today's society we are becoming less dependent on cash use and more on plastic or electronic payments. There are many ways to accept credit and debit payments, now you should review the fees for use of these various services. There are many companies that offer the availability to process credit/debit cards and other services which may benefit your business. The fees you will be paying should be reviewed at least annually, as your business grows there may be a better option for your credit/debit card processing.

Does your business require inventory for self-use or warehousing materials for purchase? How much will you need and what will the cost be? This initial investment needs to be in your startup budget. However, it's not just the inventory but also the systems to hold the inventory and the tracking system to know when to reorder. These would all be costs factored into the startup budget.

What about the intellectual property? A lot of discussion is taking place around this who owns the rights of intellectual property. Do you have proprietary systems or programs that need to be protected, such as a trademark, or have you created a product that needs a patent? Obtaining patent and copyright protections are a special need, seek out an attorney who specializes in this type of work. The investment varies from firm to firm and pricing can start around $2000 plus filing fees. Should you need to do this process include the investment in the startup budget.

Chapter 8: Funding Your Business

Starting and running a business is a tedious job. Many people don't follow their dream because of it. Yet others are not deterred and go through the planning process only to realize that they need money to get started. Some will quit before they even investigate how to get funding. I don't want this to be you.

Borrowing money can be a scary process. Most people haven't dealt with business funding and the fear of the unknown takes hold. This chapter will help prepare you and lessen that fear.

Before we dive into the process let's dispense some myths associated with business funding.

Myth: Funding = Success.
Reality: Not every successful business borrows money and not every business that borrows money achieves long-term success.

Myth: Funding will give my business stability.

Reality: If you are not generating adequate revenue, your funding will be depleted, and your business will be on rocky ground.

Myth: Investors have my best interest in mind.
Reality: You may find that some investors will help and take on a mentor roll for you and your business. Remember that ultimately investors care about a return on their investment. They have different ideas than you do.

Myth: I can just get a business loan.
Reality: New businesses may find it difficult to get a loan because they have no business history, credit history or experience. Lenders may want a large down payment or charge a higher interest rate to balance the risk if they do give a you loan.

These aren't meant to scare you, but rather eliminate some of the thinking that we've all heard. Having those out of the way, I want to provide you with information that will help you if you do need to obtain funding for your business.

What are some of the ways to fund a business?

Funding is generally categorized in two ways:

1. Equity – Using the business or funds that do not have to be repaid or reported. This type of loan is listed on the positive side of a balance sheet.
2. Debt – These are funds that must be repaid, such as loans. These are found on the liability side of a balance sheet.

Let's look at some of the options available to businesses starting with the equity options.

- **Bootstrapping:** Pay as you go with the revenue generated by the business.
- **Self-funding:** The name implies how this works-you use your own funds for the business. This works well if you are starting a side hustle business. You could use your personal credit to fund such as personal loan or credit cards.
- **Friends and family:** Is there anyone in your family or friends circle that can provide you with a loan? This is always a

risky option as it can cause a rift between family members or friends.

- **Angel investors:** These are individuals or groups that you can seek out who have the funds available to invest in various business. Often without many strings attached.

- **Cloud funding:** Pitching your business idea to people via the internet to find multiple investors. Be sure to research the rules and regulations around this topic before you give it a try.

- **Partners:** Bringing in a partner who, usually purchases a percentage of the business while providing cash for the business. You do give partial control of the business and the profits to your partner.

- **Venture capital:** Individuals or groups who will often help you get started or if you are in the early stages of the business. They often want a significant share of the business.

- **Crowd funding:** This is done using one of several platforms to ask for money to start your business. (i.e., Go Fund Me or Kickstarter) You will want to research the rules and regulations surrounding this option.

- o The options for you will vary by the type of industry you are in. **Always** do your homework and research your options.

Time to look at the other side of the balance sheet, Debt options.

- **Banks and credit unions:** These are your traditional lenders and requirements vary by institution.
- **SBA loans:** The Small Business Administration (SBA) has several programs that you can look into to determine what fits your business best. They do not give loans directly, but rather provide a loan guarantee to traditional lenders. Using the SBA loan process may have looser requirements than the traditional lender without the SBA guarantee.

- **Small Business lenders:** There are an array of businesses that loan to small businesses. They generally require collateral for the loan, so be sure to read the contract carefully as the terms can be wide-ranging and the loan could end up costing you more money than you thought.

What do I need to know before applying for a business loan?

Nobody wants to be denied for a loan. Doing your homework and learning about the entire loan process can increase your chances of getting your loan. Here are some points to take notes on before you apply:

1. **How much money will I need?**
   We covered this in the budget portion of the business plan in Chapter 3. You will need to show the need for the money and how your revenue exceeds the loan requested.

2. **Check your credit score.**
   You are borrowing money for the business, and the fact is, YOU are the

business. The higher your credit score, the better terms you may qualify for. Review your credit report for errors as they can have an adverse effect on you and your business. If you are already in business, make sure you review the business credit history.

3. **Have a solid business plan**.
The business plan is the foundation for your business and shows funders how profitable it will be. It is vital to have a well thought out and professionally presented plan.

4. **Talk to a business mentor or hire a consultant to look at your plan**.
Your need to have your plan reviewed by a business mentor for flow, completeness or anything that could be adjusted to provide a better picture of your business. Your other option is hiring a consultant to do the review, and this is a service that we offer. If you are interested in having us provide a review email me at dave@businessplananswerman.com.

What will I need to apply for a business loan?
The lender will have an application you complete. The information that you will need to fill out or have supporting documents to verify is:

- Personal information
  - Previous addresses
  - Other names you have used
  - Any criminal record details
  - Educational background
- Resume
  - Not just yours, but also any other business principal owners must include theirs.
- Business plan
  - A complete, solid, and detailed plan including projections as described in Chapter 3.
- Income tax returns
  - Three years of personal and business tax returns.
- Loan history
  - Any loans your currently have or that have been paid off in the past six months.

- Bank statements
  - One year of personal and business statements
- Collateral
  - This will vary by funder and the type of business.
- Use of loan
  - How will you be using the loan proceeds.
- Debt schedule
  - A list of all of your debt-personal and business. This includes collateral, secured or unsecured, monthly payments, and balance.
- Legal documents
  - Business license and registration
  - Building lease (current or proposed)
  - Business information
  - Articles of incorporation or LLC filings
  - IRS letter with EIN
  - Copies of any contracts such as subsidiaries or affiliates
  - Copies of any franchise agreements

How do I choose a lender?

Choosing a lender is like hiring an employee. You need to interview them and ask some questions to find one that you're comfortable working with and that will lend money to businesses in your industry. I always say start with the banks that you have established relationships with and that know you. You should ask some questions about them and the loan process. Here are some suggestions:

- Do you loan to businesses in my industry?
- What are the interest rates and loan costs?
- What is the payment schedule?
- When will the first payment be due?
- How long will the loan process take after the application is submitted?

You may have had to speak with several lenders to find the right fit. When reviewing your notes from the conversations that you will have with the various lenders, there are some other things to consider as you decide on one:

- Eligibility requirements
  - Minimum credit score required
  - Minimum years in business

- o Minimum annual revenue
- Loan Options
  - o Loan Type
    - Fixed rate
    - Adjustable rate
    - Fixed amount
    - Line of credit
    - Maximum lending amount
    - Repayment terms available
  - o Cost associated with the loan
    - Annual percentage rate (APR)
    - Down payment
    - Loan application fee
    - Underwriting fee
    - Closing cost
    - SBA loan guarantee fee
    - Any additional fees
  - o What are the loan restrictions?

What do lenders look for?
The 5 C's of credit

Character - **Your willingness to pay back your loan**

- Lenders are interested in your payment history. How you have paid your bills in the past is an indication of how you will pay your future debt obligations.
- Lenders are interested in a pattern of repayment.
- Since lenders don't know you, your credit score tells a lender how you will pay your business loan.
- Credit scores vary among the three major credit reporting agencies. Contact them all and request your credit report with a credit score.
    - o Experian: www.experian.com
    - o Equifax: www.equifax.com
    - o Transunion:www.transunion.com
- Also log on to www.annualcreditreport.com
- Lenders also consider what experience you have in the industry in which you

want to start a business.

Cash flow - Your capacity to pay back your loan

- Lenders are interested in your ability to pay back debt.
- Global or universal cash flow is the amount of cash available from all sources of income m relationship to the total amount of business and personal debt.
- Debt service coverage calculation:

$$\frac{\text{Business Income + Personal Income}}{\text{Business Debt + Personal Debt}}$$

- Translation: For every \$X in total sources of income, you have no more than \$1 in total debt. This is only a guideline.
- Definition of debt: 12 months of principal and interest payments on such things as your exist in g business loans, personal or business mortgage payments, minimum credit card payments, car loans, boat loans, vacation property mortgages, or

anything that appears on your credit report.

Collateral - How lenders get paid if the business fails
- Lenders value collateral at liquidation rates, meaning that they discount collateral based on the useful life of the asset being pledged.
- Lenders require a 1:1 ratio, meaning that for every dollar you want to borrow, you should have a dollar's worth of liquidated value of collateral.
- If there is insufficient collateral, lenders may look to personal assets to secure the loan.

Capitalization - How much money you must put into the business
- Lenders require that you invest non-borrowed funds into the business.
- The more non-borrowed funds you invest into the business, the less money you must borrow, and thus, the lower your monthly loan

payment.
- In existing businesses, capital also refers to the retained earnings in the business. Positive retained earnings indicate you have invested the profits into the business.

Conditions - What else is out there that can affect my ability to repay the loan?
- Make sure your lender is aware of the economic, regulatory, geographic, and industry conditions that may positively or negatively affect your business.

Now that you know the various ways to fund your business, I can hear you mumbling, "that's more than I wanted to know." But being knowledgeable about the process can help speed things up and reduce the time it may take you to get the funds you need.

Preparation is a key piece of business. You've put a lot to thought and hard work into your planning process to get to this point, so going into a lender meeting unprepared can give them the impression that you're not professional and you don't want that. You need to present your plan and yourself as professionally as possible.

Chapter 9: Closing Thoughts

This book has given you critical information to help you decide if starting a business is the right move for you and your idea. Do you feel nervous or anxious about creating your business plan? I can help you. If you would like us to review your plan when you have completed it, assist you along the way, or even write the plan for you, schedule a time to talk to me. Here is the link to my calendar, https://calendly.com/businessplananswerman/30min.The steps I shared are those from lessons learned from my 30+ years as an entrepreneur and business owner. My goal is to save you time and money by sharing these lessons unless you have 30 years to learn on your own.

Along with my experience I shared thoughts from the frequently asked questions from clients. I certainly hope you have picked up some useful information as you read through this book.

One of the key takeaways from my years of experience is that you can't reach the level of success you seek without help at some point. Whether it's a team of people working in your business, a mastermind group, or business coach. The most successful people are not afraid to reach out for help. I certainly would have not reached the level I'm at without these things.

There are many coaches out there and I suggest you interview many of them to see who the best fit for you. Before hiring someone check their references by asking for a list of some of their clients to talk to about their experiences. Think of hiring a coach a long-term investment. The same goes for mastermind groups- find the right one that will get you to where you want to go.

My business is helping entrepreneurs and business owners create their business plan using time-tested methods. Check out our website at www.businessplananswerman.com or if you have questions email me at dave@businessplananswerman.com. On our website we have resources that you may find beneficial.

Wishing you the greatest success!

Resources

Recommended books:
From the Bottom Up: The ultimate guide for business planning to profitability
    By David L Brown
Mind Capture Series by Tony Rubleski
Social Media Overload by Corey Perlman
E Boot Camp by Corey Perlman
The Closer I, II, III by Ben Gay III
Sales Closing Power by Ben Gay III
Dream Business Series by Jim Palmer
Think and Grow Rich by Napoleon Hill

Helpful links:
Online scheduler
    www.calendly.com
Information resource
    www.hubspot.com
Email marketing
    www.mailchimp.com
Email marketing
    www.constantcontact.com
Video conferencing
    www.zoom.com

Pinnacle Media Group LLC

www.pinnaclemediagroupllc.com

Credit card processing

www.square.com

Credit card processing

www.paypal.com

The Ultimate Business Start-up Checklist

- ☐ Why do I want to start a business?
- ☐ Am I willing to invest the needed time and money to build a successful business?
- ☐ Is my idea a candidate for a successful business?
    - ☐ Is there a market for my product/service?
    - ☐ Who is my preferred customer?
    - ☐ How much money will I need to earn from my business?
    - ☐ Will this business be able to generate that amount?
    - ☐ What makes my product/service different from those currently in the marketplace?
- ☐ Name of the business
    - ☐ Think about how it will be as a domain:
        - ☐ How easy is it to remember?
        - ☐ Length of the name
    - ☐ Search domain availability prior to

registering your name
- [ ] What legal entity will the business be?
    - [ ] Sole Proprietor
    - [ ] Partnership
    - [ ] Limited Liability Company (LLC)
    - [ ] Corporation
        - [ ] S-Corp
        - [ ] C-Corp
- [ ] File the required paperwork for your entity type
- [ ] Fin a business attorney
- [ ] Find a CPA/accountant
- [ ] Write your business and marketing plan
    - [ ] Include a startup budget for the one-time cost to open your business
    - [ ] Check out our website www.businessplananswerman.com for help
- [ ] Fund the business (startup loan, SBA loan, Venture Capital or other) if needed
- [ ] Choose a location for your business
    - [ ] Obtain any permits as required
    - [ ] What signage will you need?

- ☐ What is the cost?
- ☐ What is allowable by municipality?
- ☐ What will the utility costs be?
- ☐ Obtain licenses required (Federal, State or Local)
- ☐ Obtain Employer Identification Number (EIN) from IRS
- ☐ Open business bank account (s)
- ☐ Purchase internet domain; consider other domain related items and cost:
  - ☐ Hosting of domain
  - ☐ Hire someone to build website
- ☐ Have website built to fit business needs
- ☐ Create business email account (s) using your domain
- ☐ Purchase necessary business insurance
- ☐ Hire employees (if needed). Will need the following:
  - ☐ Hiring process
  - ☐ Understand labor laws if not familiar
  - ☐ Job descriptions for each position
  - ☐ Organizational chart
  - ☐ Pay scale

- [ ] Will they be employee and independent contractor (know the difference)?
- [ ] Workers compensation insurance
- [ ] Payroll system
- [ ] Set up a state withholding account
- [ ] Do your employees live in another state may need that state withholding and city withholding accounts?
- [ ] Set up a Federal UA account
- [ ] Accounting/bookkeeping system
  - [ ] Ability to accept credit cards
  - [ ] Billing system
  - [ ] Is a sales tax number required?
- [ ] Business telephone line (s)
  - [ ] If your business is in your home <u>DO NOT</u> use your home number have a separate line/number
- [ ] Create your business brand
  - [ ] Logo (best to have a graphic designer help)
  - [ ] Letterhead
  - [ ] Business cards

- ☐ Invoices (if needed)
- ☐ Brochures/ flyers
- ☐ Other advertising materials
- ☐ Identify a process to build your brand
- ☐ Social media campaign
- ☐ Advertising
- ☐ Build this into your marketing plan
- ☐ Press releases
- ☐ List who to send them to
- ☐ How will you network and what are the opportunities?
- ☐ Will any of your items/name need to be trademarked?
- ☐ Identify suppliers and vendors (if needed)
- ☐ Purchase and supplies and inventory needed to open your business
- ☐ Identify and purchase a contact relationship management (CRM) program/software

About the Author

Dave Brown is a leader in business planning. His message is designed to help entrepreneurs understand the need for a business plan and to remove the fear and pain of writing that plan. Dave is an in-demand speaker and consultant who has helped many clients write their business plans to meet the requirements of lenders and operate their business. He enjoys sharing his 30+ years' experience in owning and operating a business to save entrepreneurs time and money.

His first book *From the Bottom Up: The Ultimate Guide for Business Planning to Profitability,* is a step-by-step guide for writing a business plan in a no-nonsense format. His second book, *Journeys to Success: 21 Empowering Stories Inspired by the Success Principles of Napoleon Hill,* which was released in March of 2016 became an international bestseller. Both books have received stunning reviews from a wide range of leaders in the business, marketing, and sales world.

His work has been featured on Blog Talk Radio, Bold Radio, Partners in Success, and Journey to Success Radio

Other Books by David Brown

A no-nonsense step by step guide for writing a business plan.

Available at https://amzn.to/2xEMSee

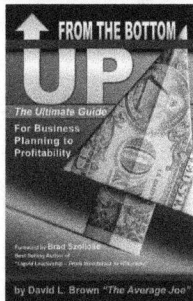

What you are actually holding in your hands is more than a book, but a powerful tool, that if you choose to take advantage of the wisdom in its pages will bring you more success than you could imagine. Why? Because Dave has removed the mystery of business planning at a time when we need it most. He has taken complex information and brought it down to earth for the regular guy. It is a guidebook. A Business Bible for a new wave of business owner. And isn't that what you want in a business advisor? Available and unpretentious, down-to-earth and no nonsense? So, start your quest in creating a business that you are proud of. And I beg you, use this book wisely. Take advantage of the man who has given you his time and expertise and connect with Mr. Dave Brown." **Brad Szollose - Award winning and International best-selling author of:** *Liquid Leadership: From Woodstock to Wikipedia—Multigenerational Management Ideas That Are Changing the Way We Run Things.*

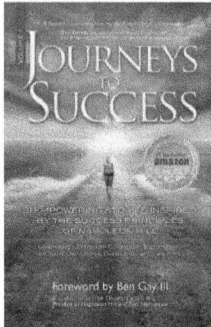

21 empowering stories of everyday people from all walks of life based on the success principles of Napoleon Hill.

Available at https://amzn.to/3aOfmRD

David Brown takes you on a stunning journey that captivates his audience. David provides his transparency of walking his talk and provides you the hope and inspiration of "YOU can do it too", no matter what life throws at you. We all have obstacles; it just depends on how we re-act or respond to them. We either allow the fears and distractions paralyzed us or re-align our direction to become stronger and more confidence.

Kim Boudreau Smith
CEO Bold Radio & KBS Publishing
Kim@kimboudreausmith.com

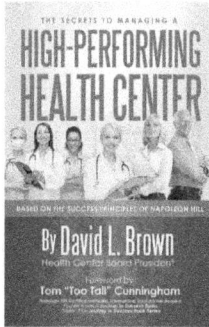

Applies the 17 success principles of Napoleon Hill to the work of a board of directors.

Available at https://amzn.to/3bOgBAj

In introducing us to Napoleon Hill's "17 principles of success," David Brown's book provides today's health center governing boards a great roadmap that can help them to lead their health care organizations to greatness.

Claudia Green Gibson
Executive VP for Communications
National Association of Community Health Centers